Dare I Disturb the Universe?

Poetic short stories and monologues

by Jaimes Lewis Moran

SEAWARK PRESS

LONDON & LEEDS

Published by Seawark Press, London and Leeds, 2016

1st edition published by the Seacroft Community Literature
and Art Society 2014, 2nd edition 2015

Copyright © Jaimes Lewis Moran 2014

Layout and typesetting by C.J. Schüler Editorial
Cover illustration by Sheila Bell of Halton, Leeds

A CIP catalogue record for this book is available from the British Library

ISBN 978-0-9935906-0-3

http://www.elfm.co.uk
https://seacroftliteratureandart.wordpress.com

Introduction

Most of this writing was developed during my treasured time with East Leeds FM's Associate Writing Group and workshops, which encourage young people of all ages to get involved and develop their own unique writing styles through informal writing days and projects.

Thanks also to the Seacroft Community Literature and Art Society.

Warning: some of the recurring themes in this book are of individualism, injustice and romance.

Dedicated to Peter Spafford, East Leeds FM's Director of Words.
The English teacher I never had, but always wanted.
He taught me well…

Contents

Every word must be heard

Every word must be heard as if the last in existence
as if the world has been in silence forever,
And the universe was still.

Waiting for that spark of inspiration, and the first act of vocal creation
From the first sounds to ever pass your lips.
They float on the wind while the cosmos listens
To your tale of lament or joy, about all things underappreciated.

It is the ability to create stories with words that should be cherished
And remembered
With their intertwined stories of wisdom and warning to the appreciative ear
So eager to listen and visualise the plot.
Oh, to laugh with joy at their stories or humour
And their struggle for what, entertainment!

Every word must be heard never truly forgot
Or else we may as well deny creation itself!

All things are related in the pursuit of creation
They seek to be immortal in many ways.
But none are more fulfilling then the arts
Be it visual, audial or sensual.

Every word must be heard as if the world has been in silence forever...

Dare I disturb the universe?

Can I create a permanent mark upon the earth?

Do I dare disturb the universe?
That vast horizon of wonder with endless possibilities.

Or will my efforts get much notice as insects do to humans.
Am I a simple insignificant speck of dust upon time?

Why do I persist against the tide of existence?
Do I dare disturb the universe with an act so huge!
That none can escape it and the universe must then take heed of me.
Dare I disturb the universe and existence, as much as it does to me?

Cans are the stones of the future

They tried to warn us with TV adverts and signs
Clean up your act before it's too late they said.

Did anyone listen...

You try to justify waste with logic and jokes
But you won't be laughing when no one comes to clear up your mess!
Just imagine passing the same litter on the street for years to come
You get older; then become fatter on your ignorance.

Maybe you're one of the lucky ones, with a family of you own.
But then you realise that there is nowhere safe to play
Due to the litter you left, and the sharp cans on the street.

Ages of rust and decades will pass, cans become the stones of the future.
Until fifty years have gone and they become dust.

Is it vain?

When someone prepares themselves for the sole purpose of satisfying
another's needs
Is it vain if they do the same?
I don't care about how anyone else in the world perceives me, except you.

And should my image be distasteful
Or anything I do to you my love become unappealing,
Then tell me the reasons why, otherwise how would I know?
People change themselves in relationships for each other
And become mature with an experience, which in turn alters mentality.
Changing minor traits is normal, changing a whole person is wrong.
Unless the change was their personal choice in the first place.

Stop hitting everything Dave! (S.H.E.D.)

Brutally beating the shed to find the tools he needs
What he needs is an attitude adjustment, not spanners!
Once he goes into that defensive mode of his, nothing gets through...
I'm not surprised too, considering how people treat him.

He doesn't deserve the abuse he gets based on bad bus conductors,
he isn't one.

He treats people with respect, waits patiently for them to reach the bus
before he departs
He doesn't speed off like others.
He truly understands that customers are more important than average
speeds and timetables.

But the passengers don't treat him kindly, which would wear any good
person down...

So for his sake, next time when you meet a bus driver
Remember to smile and be nice.

* * *

I know you have a condition of always pushing things away,
But that won't solve anything will it?
The harder you push or try to pull me away,
The more adamantly I refuse to let you go.
So stubborn and full of pride!
Drop the masculine mentality,
And don't be afraid to be vulnerable.

Behold: the next generation!

And oh, how I look on with distant distaste
My very essence despises you,
You, who have youth & security,
Oh, how I'd love to break your walls down with reality.
Enjoy those 19years o' bliss because after that it's all downhill
And how it makes me ooze with joy come judgment day.
With your lack of subtlety, ignorant to the ways of charm and honour.
Look at these masters of vulgarity as they spit on the arts,
With a language of grunts and flemm.

Oh, how society has fallen...
What is it about you that makes me burn with fury
From whence did my inferno of hate spring forth?
And consume my conscience and patience!
And how I have fallen with despair
Behold the next generation, and see how society has progressed.

Significantly highlighted, enjoy drunk! (S.H.E.D.)

Stumbling home under the moonlight
Falling asleep on the doorstep with the stars above you

Then, waking up to the roaring of birds and traffic!
With the cool cats and shaggy dogs*
(*that is not a reference to one night stands or people)

Ah alcohol, what an obsession to have!
So very significantly highlighted by a society obsessed with it

Cooking with wine, drinking it while you cook, why not!
Wasting your university grant to get wasted, DEAL!
Sloppy, slurping singing and guitar playing, I've been there...

Alcohol, enjoy it while you can...

Rachael fights back!

Against anything and everything in the world
That lacks the sense to see its faults,
It's wrong motives, flawed beliefs and bad music tastes.
Rachael fights back!
And takes a stand before the increasingly mindless tide
Of teen idols, boy bands and the normal!
Rachael fights back from a life of dull normalness
And refuses to conform as she leads the revolution,
While becoming the dreaded, woman, with opinions!
Rachael fights back against any and all that would have her blindly follow;
She is the black sheep and stands defiantly in the face of her adversity.
Rachael does not cower or hide.
No, Rachael tenaciously fights back with every atom in her body
Against the fabricated template of a teenager
The false portrayals, their complicatedness and intellect reduced
With music taste restricted to the charts.
She is off the charts with rage, and will not let this stand
So, Rachael fights back!

Heart condition

She's got a condition.
The one where she cares too much about her family
And goes out of her way more than she should.
She's got a condition.
Where her heart contains so much love
And is willing to share it with anyone,
A condition that will only get worse and increases by day.
She's got a condition of unconditional love.
But that is the burden of being a mum
And a sensitive, caring soul.

Join anything, do anything

What do you expect to happen if you never participate?
It's okay to tell people you like what they have done, you know.
Don't be embarrassed of sharing you interests, for instance here's mine!

Yes, I know it's a book...
And you don't like reading but humour me
Tell me what you think of these words?

Could you relate to the characters and situations?
Or did it make you angry that I wrote this much without your help.

* * *

Join anything you can
Exhaust all possible options and push the limits of imagination,
Before you grow bitter and old like me.
Do anything you can to stay innocent and young at heart,
Enjoy every sacred moment as if it were your last till
The marrow of life is dry.
Only then will you be left with great love, people and stories.

The sunlight walks away

The sunlight walks across the hills of home
Bringing radiance and life to Scotland.

Aye, any sign of it will be cherished indeed
Before the decent into darkness begins anew,
With its cruel voice and forceful blows against any in the way.

* * *

Everyone runs to safety but the sunlight walks away.
I travel out into the wilderness braving the elements of cold rain and wind
My journey is never over though,
Because tomorrow I will find myself once more in a struggle against death.

I will defy the people who say it can't be done – living in such a desolate place.

It's a harsh life living on the moors but someone must do it
Because it's the only way to prove to them that people can live anywhere
But only with the right reasons and true Yorkshire stubbornness.

Juliet waits...

Upon the balcony
Gazing up at the constellations she feels small and insignificant,
But most of all, lonely...
Because the planets have the sun and the stars
To embrace each other in the vast horizon of space.
Yet where is the Lover she desires?
And can he sense her longings for kindness and warmth
On those cold barren nights.
Where hope is extinguished, and lost so easily to darkness.
 Juliet waits for her Romeo on the balcony, as Romeo climbs up to her.
(To be continued...)

Anything but poetry!

It's so full of pretentious, stuck up words created by and for snobs,
Who believe they are above anyone else who owns a pen,
Or doesn't have a degree in writing.
Anything at all, anything but poetry.
And for heaven's sake it doesn't even rhyme!

* * *

Anything but poetry, that goes on and on
For pages until someone gives up
And loses their motivation to read,
Or in some cases, falls asleep...

Anything but poetry, full of riddles and complicated wisdom
Packaged wrong for the average reader who needs simplicity!

I've heard that poetry is the art of describing beauty
Or the language used to woo women with cunning and hidden agendas,
I believe it is about telling the simple truths of life?

And the truth is poetry makes my head hurt...

It keeps me up at night trying to decipher its true meaning

Tell me anything but poetry – a declaration of love
Give me anything but words – a deeply desired kiss

And a future that our dead poets wrote of, but were painfully denied...

My city (Leeds)

How you call to me in nightlife gloom illuminated by street lights
I see the people struggling to get home at night
Stumbling down your endless labyrinth of streets.
Your presence in the morning with a warm halogen glow
Brings days of summer to mind
Which leaves me ready for what is, what can & what will come today.
As I travel towards you, your shadow looms over me growing bigger
Until it eventually overwhelms me!
But it doesn't send fear into my heart?

Instead I eagerly await and look forward to our long overdue embrace
It's been mere hours since we've parted, and how I long to see your face.
Despite my efforts to know your every corner, place and crevice
I find myself incomplete.
Because no matter how much I search look or seek
You always have more unknown hidden stories, treasures
                                          and secrets for me.

Lost interests

Why do people lose the interest to question the world?
Why do they accept things at face value instead of objecting
                                                    to a subject?
Doing as they are told, doing the same as the person next to them
So eager to fall in line with the rest of them!
Well, I refuse!
Refuse to lose my interest and my thirst to know more
To know why, why are things the way they are?
Why that colour, that shape.
That functionality which no one questions and says:
I could make it better than that!
I have a simple idea that no one has attempted yet
Which you call silly, stupid, pointless and impossible,
But it's only impossible if no one is willing to try!
Try to do better, Try to think outside the box
Of these four walls and corners that we reside in.

Try to be, and think different.

I refuse to lose my childlike interests for fun, life
And thingy things that catch my eye.
The stuff which you call mundane, completely refuse
And ignore unashamedly.

Men have emotions!?

Get over it.
We like agonisingly romantic films and emotional characters
Who we can relate to such as James dean.
Who was one of the first men in moving pictures to show
That it was okay to be vulnerable,
Why should we be ashamed of that!
As for expressiveness through words, the fault lies in advertising.
Stay there! Look good and don't say anything at all.

Women talk a lot about their opinions not being heard
But what about a different notion on masculinity
From the perspective of a straight guy.
I've known women who are more likely to watch action films than men.
And those men, secretly pine for romantic films and cuddles.
We are not robots, nor are we made of stone.
Never make us ashamed of our emotions in any situation
Especially the ones with three pure words.
We are modern men!
(Feelings included in the package of: brains, body and balls!)

The East Leeds FM Methodist chapel (Chapel-FM)

Here at last, the wait is over
The dust has settled and all is right with the world.

My relief is indescribable
My excitement overwhelming to both my speech patterns
                                    and movements.
I stumble and fall over myself to find the words
These words to describe my joy!
At last the dream is real and not just an idea any longer
But transformed into something physical
On many senses to behold, to smell and touch.
Here at last – my hopes fulfilled.
Here at last – at home.
Here at last – in the chapel.

Mi amore (My love)

I have known you for years, but you have never seemed more perfect
Your eyes have captivated my soul, and your mind has my heart.

Every second spent with you has enriched my life.
If my time is required, I'll give every second to you
If you need any love, then every drop of it is yours.

Whatever you desire, I will get
Anything to make you smile, and never forget my love for you.
I would do anything at all, everything for love
Because you brought me a reason to live, by loving you.
I would do anything at all, everything for love
And especially for you.

Was it worth the pain?

Of a strained heart and mind
To fall apart and piece yourself together once more
Only to find yourself fragile, but stronger than before.
Was it worth it?
Knowing that you may fail or succeed.

I fear not failing, but the unknown of success.
I am scared they may appreciate me,
Or worse want more!
Was it worth the pain?
While you gained drugs and sordid pleasure from addiction
In doing so, you lost everyone and everything that matters.
Was it worth the pain of seeing all your friends die?
Over a small piece of land!
Was it for personal victory or our freedom?
Was it worth the pain?
Sometimes no, others yes...
But I learned from it, whether I liked it or not
It changed me, into who I am today.
Was it worth it all, maybe…
Was it worth the insults?
Both mental and physical from twisted people and children
Who treated me like an outcast, yes!
Because of them I know the kind of person to be
I learnt to express myself through words,

And now I get revenge in a positive way.

I love you more...

How competitive four words can be
Is it wrong to say so?
When everyday my thoughts drift heaven bound towards you
And I fear that you love me,
But not as much as I bestow upon you…
Can such a fraction of love survive?
Would it increase or fade away?
And I find irrational fears take hold of me
When another catches your gaze, Seeking to steal you away...

I love you more
Every second, as hours turn into days,
Alas I cannot imagine the same…

Slumber of ignorance

Wake up from your slumber of ignorance
And take some notice won't you!
Why don't you question the world that resides in front of thee?
Are you completely blind, and oblivious to the miracles of time
                                        that exist!

Why are you void of wonder?
So empty and uninterested,
Is it due to you excessive focus on thyself?
Wake up from this slumber of ignorance
So that you may cherish this day and life,
Then finally at last, you will live!

But then again,
If ignorance is bliss, tis folly to be wise...
Why should I be wise I wonder, and let you have all the fun?

I've never lived, only existed

I'm fractured, both inside and out like shards of glass
I've never lived, only existed...

The world passes by like dust in the wind
While I stay still, in status
Unmoved and immobile like a statue.
My family worry about me, but worry never cured depression.

I've been told to seek help, to grow up, and move on.

But those emotions regarding you are burned into my essence
Nothing else matters, not even my own welfare,
I lived only for you.

But with your absence
I feel void and empty of purpose.
I've been told to seek help, to grow up and move on.
But my reason for existing was you.
And now I find myself without.

To wake beside you

Would be the most pure scene
To see your eyes open as they stare upon me.

Oh, to watch you sleep innocently in serenity
You look so blissful and content.
I love and will cherish the essence of you eternally
Because being beside you leaves me in peace,
And for now the world can wait.
For in this fraction of time
This paradise of affection,
All that exists and all that I see
Is you and me, together at last, alone.

* * *

Don't go, stay here with me.

Staring affectionately

I'm not staring at the walls
Or looking at the mess of clothes on the floor,
Because you are the only subject I seek.
You captivate my gaze with your eyes,
My soul and atoms ache to be closer to you
As you stare intensively from across the room.
I'm not staring at the world around us,
Cause the only thing that exists is you.

* * *

What does that look mean, she asks?

a.   It means I need you more than you will ever know.
b.   It says stop talking, start kissing me.
c.   You must be kidding, surely you know by now?

Unwanted, unloved (book)

They call you old and outdated,
Unwanted and unloved.
They look straight through you
Or walk on by, as if you were never there
And never mattered to anyone other than yourself.

And you question:
Why does no one care about me?

* * *

You know that feeling,
That emotion you feel when you are dragged to despair
When the world ignores you, denies your existence,
Then calls you, useless.

To me its half hate, and half sadness...

Hate – that they are stuck in a world where a cover is more important
than its content,
And sadness that they will never know the fire they are fuelling
inside your core.

To be reckless, bold and immature

I want to be reckless, not restrained by patience
No second thoughts to actions blocking me.

Would it be so wrong for me to act on impulse?
Regardless of the outcome, to hell with the consequences!
At least for once in my life...
I want to love with abandoned
Take leaps of faith into the unknown,
Do all the wrong things
And have the courage to take the plunge.
I want to believe in hope above all gloom and despair
And see a bright future
Due to the immaturity that led me there.

With someone who isn't afraid of romance
Or being vulnerable like me.

The first step (mentally)

Was a struggle...

My mind, feet and heart resisted
So weary of what lies ahead,
The uncertainty of the outcome, I was filled with dread.
Dreading that I was destined for something greater
Or doomed to fail from the start.
I feared the unknown.

But for better or worse I must carry on!
If not for my dreams
Then for all those who courageously believe in their ambitions
To become and achieve so much more.
More than a person,
A story, a legend.

So great that time itself will bow in awe
With how you spent such a short time on earth.

But first I must be brave and take the first step.

Do I dare to?
Will I?
Can I?

An overlord's view of the supermarket

Look at those people running around like specs upon the earth
In the scramble for provisions and products.

With the announcement of a discount, Chaos ensues
And I stand above in control of everything.

I see all
My multiple eyes and spies surround you,
My gaze on every shopper and isle.
I will steal your soul and image should you choose to steal from me!
(Ha ha – etc.)

There will be full prosecutions and no prisoners at all!

* * *

Big brother sees a sister stealing in the mall.
Who was warned by the signs she didn't see at all.
Those in plain sight, residing on the floor
Yet she wishes she had when the cage falls/slams down on her as she
exits...

(To be continued)

I ain't dead!

What makes you say that?
I've been biding my time for the right moment to emerge.

Oh, the look on you faces!
You thought I was shy and mundane
It never crossed your mind
The possibility that I had talent, did it?
That I have potential, and a voice to shout against those nay-sayers.

And now the time has come, for me to voice my opinions.
(I've been waiting years to say my piece)
Just because I was quiet, doesn't mean I am still now,
Even though I felt empty because of you.
I ain't dead!

I'm just keeping my mouth shut while I digest the insults which:
Sustain me and fuel the words I fire back!

She hates chocolate...

The over-expensive cost
That bloated sickly feeling afterwards.
She hates chocolate.
And says the mere smell makes her increase in weight
Which is preposterous either way.
How could such a thing happen?
Does the aroma contain magic?
Or a curse that defies the laws of reason!
I devour a piece, and then it goes straight to my hips
As she watches on
In laughter and pure unadulterated astonishment.

Well, she did warn me!

Serendipity

Does fate have a sense of humour?
It must have because the way we met was a joke!
We collided in the train due to lack of space
Therefore were unable to escape each other's gaze,
So close to each other…
Face to face, we cannot turn our faces away in shame
So embarrassed by the way we stared at each other.
In a compact space we felt confined
Without privacy or breathing space.
And then your warm breath reaches my face
Which leaves me with no place to look, or move
Except closer toward you,
And then I do nothing, but regret…

(To be continued)

Suddenly, he exits dangerously (S.H.E.D.)

Throwing caution to the wind like so many scattered bank notes
Ready to start anew, to once more live without possessions.

They will never own me he declares,
I am free at last!
No more costly fees for maintaining or owning a vehicle
My feet will take me there!
No more overpriced insurance for things that I no longer have
Like a house…..
He hesitates in fear...
Where will I live?
Who will employ me while I am homeless?
What about my future,
Do I even have one now….

Steven: he exists dangerously without thinking of the consequences...

(To be continued)

Study her emotions and desires (S.H.E.D.)

Study her emotions and desires
Her affection, interests, and what she loves or hates
Through her body language.

Only then can you even begin to comprehend her thought processes
Which are constantly in turmoil?
And even then you will never understand her
For a woman is the greatest mystery of all time!

* * *

I believe that many politicians in parliament are groomed to deal with
'male' competitors.
Isn't it wonderful when females face those same career politicians?
Because they don't know how to react, and the rule book gets destroyed!

Justice absent

Same old scenario
Corruption in the police
Failed politics and groups
That are never given the chance to do an alternative.
Where is their chance to do right?
And make us proud of their endeavour.
The rich get rich,
While the poor get poorer.
Because the wrong people are in charge of our country.

Vote for a clean conscience and common sense
Not for a majority or hatred of another party
Regardless of how they conduct their policies and themselves

Vote for what you believe in
Not because of family/peer pressure.

Death as a keen fencer

You can duck and weave
Parry or counter attack with every muscle and grain of life inside of you.

But none can escape the damage that death will deal in due time.
That sudden blow, a surprise attack!
The delayed reaction leading up to the end.

You can avoid him/her/it
But not forever the sharp point and touch of death.
No armour can shield you from it
Acceptance is the only choice.

Listening to silence

I am listening to silence
So scarce and sacred in these modern times
So cherished and precious, it's such a rarity I find.

If only such things would last.
Alas/yet such things do not endure the trials of time.

I am listening to silence, excluded from the world outside.
I am sick of the noise, the voices that never retreat.

Oh, how the world has become so loud, everything shouts.
The words scream in print
And the pictures demand utter attention from the viewer.

* * *

(Quietly) I am listening to silence,
Because the world is too loud…
I'm sorry if you didn't hear me, I'll say it again…
For the people in the back row, for the people just arriving in this venue
And for the people out there in the street.
(LOUD!!!)
I am listening to silence,
Because the world is too loud!!!

A book locked away

What use is a book of wisdom without eyes to read its pages?
As it's stored in a sterile place unknown and untouched.

Let the books be free I say!
Because books were meant to be held, and read in eager abandoned.
By all means, digitise those words for many to discover in these new modern times
But let a book be read and read, until all that remains is the cover.

That is the destiny of the written page
Unlike an unloved toy on a shelf, they will be used until decayed.

That is how it should be, Cherished until their final days.

So please take these books eagerly and read, and read again.
Then give me what I deserve, appreciation!

Why were they proud?

Why were they proud in the first place?
Why are you proud of your deeds?
Why in the name of glory were they proud!
During the blitz in our hour of need.

Why, because they stood against the tide, unflinching
While death roared on!
And they roared back with just as much volume and force
Then anyone ever dared to use in the name of justice.

Why should you be proud of the past?
Because everything you know
Nay, everything is owed to it
Everything around you came from it, and is tied to it intrinsically.

Those pioneers who had small ideas
Motivated by dreams and fun!
That had such impact to culture in many definitions.

You will never know, how much you owe
Or how much you will need, your past.

Let me build!

Show me a barren land that no one loves,
I will cherish it, and bring it back to life with attentive love.
I can nurse it back to health with water and toil.
Give me seeds and I will grow a garden,
A garden that is so momentous and pure
That it will be seen from space.
Hand me a brick to place upon this green land
So that I may create a home for lovers of nature and life.
Let me build it, with my two hands.
Let me build it, and they will come to see
And live among the gardens and trees of Babylon.
A land that legends told of.
A place that began, with a dream.
Then after my years of effort, scatter my ashes around these trees.

Let me build a community of tightly wound friendship
With stubborn roots reaching far and wide, crawling for miles,
One that will outlast all other metal creations and places,
Places born of ill conceived purpose.
Let me build a home with purpose
Oh, please let me build it soon.
Please, let me build the home of my dreams.

Bridlington beach (my first visit in twelve years)

I had forgotten everything about you
My memories were lost as I grew up,
Yet here I am twelve years later fully grown, old and wise.

I feel drowsy due to the travel sickness tablets I have taken.

Inside the car I am rocked to sleep
By a terrain of bumps, holes and hills,
While the sun bears down in a UV shade of blue.

The surface of the sea reflects the soft white clouds of cotton
While the shimmering silver seas turn quietly in the distance.

I feel warm rays of sun upon my face which leaves me contently relaxed
Aside the eerie silence of the beach during school hours.

Then I take the sequences of the sand along the beach.

I remove my shoes and feel the earth beneath me
As if it was the first time ever.
We are once more in contact like old friends
Who were separated long ago unfairly, without reconciliation,
Until now at last we are together.

It started with the sink and slide of my feet into the sand,
Although as I walk it changes quickly
Into sharp shells, glass and crisp crunchy seaweed.

Then I walk upon flat snake trails atop hard wet sand
Which feels like walking upon fresh carpet elsewhere.

Bridlington beach – part two: the depart

But then suddenly as I get to the end
I am met by ice bucket challenge type water
Which starts at my ankles and as it increases
I get a sense of impeding nausea
From the conquest of invading waves attacking me.

Then I slowly march up to the stairs leading away
From this great divide, this otherworldly place.

After all that I dry myself
And put on my concrete shoes one more,
They tie me to the earth, but keep me apart from it

I'll miss this.

Prove it!

Prove to me, that you can perform live
Otherwise, get out!

Yes, right here, right now…

A singer, actor or dance artist must be ready for instantaneous
                                                    entertainment
Regardless of the setting or time!

And the time is now!
Take this small moment and make it epic.

Don't be shy, show us your skills!

Don't be afraid, of being heard or seen,
The world is waiting, as are we.

And if you don't try at all, you are wasting our time...
You say you have talent, prove it!